D1565583

CARS

CARS

Marjorie Eberts
Martha Eberts

VGM Career Horizons
a division of NTC Publishing Group
Lincolnwood, Illinois USA

Dedication

To Shari, who delights in short car trips exploring scenic areas.

Photo Credits:
Pages 1, 29, 43, 57, and 71: Photo Network, Tustin, CA.
All other photographs courtesy of the authors.

Library of Congress Cataloging-in-Publication Data

Eberts, Marjorie.
    Career Portraits, cars / Marjorie Eberts, Martha Eberts.
      p.   cm. — (VGM's career portraits)
    Includes index.
    Summary: Discusses career opportunities for car enthusiasts
including auto repair, design, driving, and customizing.
    ISBN 0-8442-4370-1
    1. Automobile industry and trade—Vocational guidance—
Juvenile literature. [1. Automobile industry and trade—
Vocational guidance. 2. Vocational guidance.] I. Eberts, Martha.
II. Title. III. Series.
HD9710.A2E2 1995   94-42627
629.2'023'73—dc20   CIP
                                                  AC

Published by VGM Career Horizons, a division of NTC Publishing Group
4255 West Touhy Avenue
Lincolnwood (Chicago), Illinois 60646-1975, U.S.A.

5 6 7 8 9 0 QB 9 8 7 6 5 4 3 2 1

Contents

The rush-hour traffic
I'd just as soon miss,
When caraftercarismovinglikethis.

Robert Lauher
Reader's Digest

Introduction

The United States has been called a nation on wheels. This seems a most appropriate description because about 150 million cars are on U.S. roads today. The car is far more than a means of transportation. For some, it is an office with phone and even fax. For customers of fast-food chains, it is a restaurant on wheels. For others, it is a seat in a movie theater. And for one in seven people, it means a job associated in some way with the automotive industry.

Reading this book will introduce you to careers with cars. Almost every career will involve direct hands-on involvement with cars. You'll find out about careers making, selling, servicing, and driving cars. You'll learn what it's like to teach people to drive and to handle car insurance claims. You will find out what happens on each job, the pleasures and pressures of the job, the pay, the perks, the training you'll need, and how to get started in a car career. Besides learning these basic career facts, you will read the career stories of people who are actually working right now with cars.

As you become better acquainted with car careers, you will be able to decide if you have the aptitude, skills, and personality to pursue one of these careers. You will also learn about the pioneers in the automotive industry as well as the success stories of other prominent figures associated with cars.

CAREERS IN
MANUFACTURING
CARS

S everal million cars roll off the assembly lines in the United States every year. But before they reach the end of the line, years of planning, designing, engineering, testing, and production planning have taken place for each model. The first step is always market research, which involves finding out what customers want in a car. Then a new model is proposed, and teams of designers work on creating the most appealing design. Meanwhile, engineers are busy designing and developing the more than 13,000 parts that will go in a car. This is a formidable task because all the pieces must fit together like a giant jigsaw

1

puzzle. After the final design is selected and the parts are engineered, the production engineers must plan the assembly of the new model. Prototypes must be built and tested in laboratories, highways, and proving grounds. Before final assembly of a car can begin, all the parts have to be built. The manufacturing of cars is one of the largest industries in the United States. There are jobs for engineers, designers, executives, managers, drafters, office personnel, salespeople, computer programmers—to name just some of the jobs in this giant industry. Nevertheless, the greatest number of people employed in this industry are those who assemble cars and the parts used in making cars.

What it's like to be an assembler

You are most likely to work in Michigan, Ohio, or Indiana, although other states do have facilities that manufacture cars and parts for cars. Furthermore, chances are three out of five that you will work at a company that has 1,000 or more employees. It is quite possible that you will work as part of a team. And you are likely to find yourself in a highly automated plant with robots working beside you.

Let's find out what happens on the job

Although the production of a car may take several years, the final assembly of an automobile takes only hours. The body of the car, which is already painted, will move down the assembly line to your station. The part that you are installing either will arrive at your station exactly when you need it or will be stored at your station. Depending on your task, the line may stop so your part can be installed, you may install the part while you walk along the moving line, or you may ride the conveyor belt to install your part. As soon as you have finished, you will repeat the same steps with the next car on the assembly line.

The pleasures and pressures of the job

At many factories, you will enjoy the camaraderie of working on a team. You may also rotate jobs with team members, which eliminates the boredom of doing the same work all the time. Assembly-line work conditions have improved in recent years with increased automation; however, your workplace may be noisy, repeating the same motions can cause injuries, and you may have to lift and fit heavy parts. And more work-related injuries happen in the automotive industry than other manufacturing industries. You will also have the pressure of keeping up with the pace of the assembly line.

The rewards, the pay, and the perks

One of the biggest rewards of working as an assembler is the pay—the highest in manufacturing. If you work for an auto or body manufacturer, you may start for as much as $13 an hour and be earning about $19 within 3 years. If you work the late shift, you will receive a premium. For overtime and Saturday work, you will receive $1\frac{1}{2}$ times your normal wage rate and double the wage rate for Sundays and holidays. In addition, you will receive very generous benefits, including health, life, and accident insurance; paid holidays; and pension plans.

Getting started

You can find out about jobs as an assembler at auto or body manufacturing plants. Another source of job information is a state employment office. You can also find out about openings through newspaper ads. Although you can be hired as an assembler without a high school diploma, most assemblers do have diplomas. Competition for these jobs is intense so having a diploma is a plus. Besides working at a plant that manufactures autos or auto bodies, you will find many assembly jobs at factories that manufacture auto parts and accessories.

Climbing the career ladder

Being an assembler is not a dead-end job; however, if you wish to advance, you will need more education and training. Fortunately, much of the training is available right at the plant, and manufacturers will often pay for further education at vocational schools and colleges. The next rung up the ladder from assembler in plants with a team approach is team leader, then to leader of a group, which is made up of several teams. From group leader, you can advance to being an assistant manager in charge of an area and then to manager of a floor.

Now decide if being an assembler is right for you

You have the advantage of making an excellent hourly wage as an assembler. The benefits package you receive will be most generous. And you may have performance bonuses based on the quality of cars produced at your factory. One negative to taking a job as an assembler is that the number of job openings is declining and is expected to continue to decline through the year 2005. This is largely because productivity has increased through the use of more and more automation. Nevertheless, there will be jobs to replace workers and jobs for more skilled workers such as welders and electricians.

Things you can do to get a head start

Because the demand for unskilled assemblers is declining, consider getting skills that will make you a more attractive job candidate. Having computer, electronics, welding, drafting, computer-aided design, and computer-aided manufacturing skills will give you the opportunity to become a precision assembler. Precision assemblers do work that requires a high degree of accuracy and are less likely to be replaced by increased automation. High school courses in math and science can provide a good background for future training.

Let's Meet...

Gayle Bowen
Assembly Line Worker

Gayle Bowen likes the team approach used at the auto plant where she assembles Toyota Corollas and Geo Prizms. She appreciates teamwork that goes beyond work to real friendships.

What first attracted you to a career in assembling cars?

The excellent pay appealed to me. It was much higher than my pay as a clerk in a large department store. And I knew that I could do the work because I had succeeded in all my other jobs.

How did you get your job?

A friend told me the NUMMI plant had job openings. I turned in my application, took mechanical and math tests, had an informal interview, and had blood and urine tests done—all on the same day. One week later, I was called back to take more tests. I put nuts and bolts together as fast as I could on the simulation test. Then I put tape on the side of a car to show I could line the tape up so the car could be painted. There was also a test to see if I could follow instructions exactly. The next week I went back and sat down with five people at a table, and we solved different problems together to show we could work as a team. After a personal interview and a complete physical, I got a job on the assembly line.

Tell me about your first job.

I was assigned to a five-person team that had five different jobs to do as we set windshields into cars. My first job was to put on the left side molding. The other jobs were setting the right and left sides of the windshield, putting on the right side molding, and building up the glass. We also had to go to another area and do repair work on windshields that did not pass the windshield leak test.

Did you need any special training?

Before I ever went out on the floor, there was a week of orientation where I learned about company policies and labor relations. During that time, different group leaders gave classes on standardized work and teamwork. When I went out on the floor, I spent the first hour watching how a left side molding was put on cars. I was given a manifest (a large sheet of paper with instructions for building the vehicle) to read so I would know a Corolla from a Prizm and which part each car got. Then gradually throughout the day, doing a little at a time, I learned how to do my job under the supervision of the team leader. For 3 days, the team leader stayed with me, giving help as needed. Within 60 days, I had learned all five of the team jobs. And within 90 days, I knew how to do repair work when it was needed.

What It's Like To Be on a Team

Team members know how to do all of the team jobs and actually rotate the jobs. As a team member, you have responsibility for getting your job done *and* seeing that the group gets its job done. If someone misses part of a job, you tell that person, and you also help out if anyone falls behind.

Your responsibility is to all the teams working together to build a car. If you see an earlier problem while doing your job, you pull what is called the "andon" cord. A light goes off in the area you have indicated, and the team leader for that area comes over to find out what the problem is.

Being on a team means far more than working together. We celebrate team members' birthdays, and we help each other when someone feels out-of-sorts. Team spirit can be infectious, too. If someone starts singing, everyone on the whole line joins in. This happens a lot during the holidays. It's also great to work with people from so many different cultures.

Let's Meet...

Tom Peters
Car Designer

Tom is the director of the Advanced Concepts Center, which designs leading-edge, advanced concept vehicles influenced by the California location, world trends, and lifestyles.

How did you get interested in car design?

It was during my second year of college (major—advertising illustration). I noticed an interesting orange catalog that one of the students brought to a class. As I paged through the class guide for the Art Center College of Design, I was immediately struck by photos of futuristic car models, illustrations, and product models. Wow! Like a lightning bolt, I knew this was for me. As with true love, it just hits you out of the blue and you know it's right. Up until this moment, I had no clue as to what car design was.

Did you need any special schooling or training?

Yes. After deciding I wanted to design cars, I hastily prepared a portfolio and was accepted at the Art Center College of Design in Pasadena, which offers a bachelor's degree in automotive design.

Describe a typical day at work.

Now that I am in a management position, my responsibilities have expanded. Before, my main concern was to generate design solutions. I now must lead and motivate design teams in pursuit of the best possible ideas for a wide range of projects.

What attributes do you need to be a good designer?

Good drawing skills and an understanding of three-dimensional modeling enable you to communicate your design ideas. However, I believe the most important attribute is having an intuitive design sense. I have worked with designers who were able to do beautiful drawings, but had a poor sense of design. I have also worked with designers whose technical skills were limited, but possessed an excellent sense of design. I would choose the latter any day of the week because skills can be taught—design sense is something you are born with.

Is there a lot of competition for jobs in design?

Yes, there is. Recent graduate classes from design schools have been large, and as corporate strategies continue in a downsizing mode, opportunities decrease. This is a trend, and it is usually cyclical in nature.

Describe your work environment.

It is a small, diverse staff of energetic people working in a creative environment.

Working on a Show Car

Several years ago, I was working on a prototype high-performance sports car—code named "Corvette Indy." This was a cooperative project between Chevrolet and Lotus. The car body was sent to England, in pieces, to be assembled.

I was sent to England to follow-up on the completion of the car. However, when I got there, I learned that the car was to be assembled in Italy. It was on to Italy for me. And no one on the team knew Italian!

Our initial meeting with the Italian team went very well. The interpreter understood mechanical terms, so there were no communication problems. The next day, though, was a different story. We had a less-expensive interpreter who wasn't as good, and we had to explain to the Italian team how to put together the fiberglass body (which was in boxes) as well as finish the body and interior.

In order to get the car completed, we used sign language and drew cartoons and diagrams on the body. After the car was finished, it was a work of art, but I always smiled when I saw it, because I know beneath its beautiful exterior paint were all kinds of funny drawings.

Success Stories

Henry Ford

Henry Ford founded the Ford Motor Company in 1903. At that time, cars were very expensive to make and buy. Ford wanted to be able to make a car that most people could afford. To do this, he needed to discover a faster and more efficient manufacturing process. Ford developed an assembly line where parts were brought to the workers on moving conveyor belts. This method greatly decreased the amount of time it took to assemble a car. Ford also came up with other ways to reduce production costs. With these savings Ford could lower the price of his car making it affordable to many people. Ford's assembly line method revolutionized automobile production. Also, Ford and his son, Edsel, established the Ford Foundation to give grants for educational purposes. Today, it is the world's largest foundation.

Ransom Eli Olds

Ransom Olds was a pioneer of the automobile industry. Among his accomplishments were the first automobile factory and the beginning of automobile mass production. Olds began learning about vehicles by inventing them in his father's shop. He started by building a three-wheeled steam-powered vehicle; next he made a four-wheeled version, and then a gasoline-powered one. In 1899, he established the Olds Motor Works. The company sold the curved-dash Oldsmobile that he designed. This car helped boost Americans' interest in automobiles.

Find Out More

You and automobile manufacturing and design

In making an automobile, the computer-aided design (CAD) technician designs car parts, and the assembler actually puts together the parts to build the car. Let's see if you have the qualities of a successful CAD technician.

1. I understand how automobiles are manufactured and how they work.
2. I know how to draft.
3. I am good at using computers and like to use them.
4. I do not mind making changes to my work.
5. I pay close attention to detail and do my work neatly.

Now, let's look at the qualities of a successful assembler.

1. I have taken high school shop and electronics courses.
2. I like to work with my hands and do it well.
3. I do not mind doing the same thing repeatedly.
4. I have an aptitude for mechanical work.
5. I can work at a fast pace.

Find out more about making automobiles

Get more details by writing to the human resources department of an automobile manufacturer. For general information about careers in making and designing automobiles, contact these sources:

Society of Automotive Engineers
400 Commonwealth Drive
Warrendale, PA 15096–0001

American Automobile
    Manufacturers Association
1620 I Street, NW
Washington, DC 20006

CAREERS IN
SELLING
CARS

E ach year about 25 million passenger cars are sold in the United States. Franchised dealers sell about 15 million new cars, and 10 million used cars are sold by new and used car dealers. To sell all these cars a very large work force of salespeople is needed and will continue to be needed as long as Americans' love affair with the automobile continues. Whether an automobile sales worker sells fancy imports, family vans, or used cars, the average salesperson will sell ten cars each month or more than 100 automobiles each year.

What it's like to be a car salesperson

You will be very knowledgeable about the cars sold at your workplace. This can mean knowing about cars sold by only one manufacturer, several manufacturers, or used cars. You may work indoors in a showroom or outside on a lot. You will frequently work in the evenings and on weekends because that is when customers will be shopping for cars. And it may even be necessary to work on some holidays.

Besides being an expert on cars, you will know how to satisfy customers by finding the cars they want. You will be able to detect if they are looking for performance, appearance, economy, special features, or a combination of factors. And you will be proficient in negotiating a price that will satisfy both your workplace and customers.

Let's find out what happens on the job

Customers will come to the showroom or lot where you work. You will show them several models that you think will meet their needs, being sure to comment on the specific features that may interest them. You will give some customers a test drive to show them how a particular car performs. If a customer is interested in a car, you will negotiate a price, frequently with the help of an assistant manager. Most customers do not purchase cars on their first visit and will require follow-up work to ensure a sale. Besides follow-up work, you will also spend time each day trying to find new customers.

The pleasures and pressures of the job

Being a car salesperson is a job that presents new challenges every day. You are always trying to discover new ways to sell cars. And you study constantly to learn more about the cars you sell as well as those your competitors sell.

This job can be stressful. There is the continual pressure of having to generate sales. Much of your income may depend upon how many cars you sell. Beginning car salespersons may even be graded by management on the number of cars they sell.

The rewards, the pay, and the perks

Successful car salespeople are able to earn excellent wages. How much you make usually depends upon how many cars you sell. An unbelievable number of compensation packages exists, ranging from only commission to only salary to different mixes of salary and commission. At present, there is some movement by dealers toward just paying salary. However, only 10 to 15 percent of all salespeople now receive salaries and no commissions.

While very successful car salespeople can earn more than $100,000 a year, the average income for selling new and used cars is $29,319. The high average is $44,788, and the low average is $20,632.

Getting started

You really need to be at least a high school graduate in order to get a job as a car salesperson. Because you will be dealing constantly with customers, good communication skills are an absolute necessity for this job. In addition, you need solid basic math skills to handle the negotiations and finance forms. Coursework in English, mathematics, and communication at a community college or college can be quite helpful.

Both new and used car dealers want to hire workers who have sales experience. Having a job in retail sales, whether you sell shoes, sporting goods, or hardware, gives you some of the experience employers are seeking.

Climbing the career ladder

Your first step on the ladder in car sales is as a salesperson. You typically will not receive much formal training but will learn on the job working with an assistant sales manager. The next step is to become an assistant sales manager—a position that will require you to negotiate sales with customers. As you climb on up the ladder and become a sales manager, you will make decisions on sales. At the top of the ladder is the general sales manager, who is responsible for all the employees in the sales department.

Things you can do to get a head start

Become knowledgeable about cars. Read automobile magazines to learn about the features and performance of different cars. You will need to be an expert on every feature of a number of cars when you become a car salesperson.

After you have a job, you will want to take part in the National Automobile Dealers Association's training and certification program. Through classes and home study you will learn about ethics, law, professional practices, customer satisfaction, and your state sales laws. After working as a salesperson for 6 months, you can take a test and be certified, showing that you are truly a professional in your job.

Now decide if selling cars is right for you

A great way to see how well you like sales is to get a part-time or summer job as a sales clerk in your local mall or some other store. You will quickly discover if you have an aptitude for sales. Besides, you will see if you can easily handle the disappointments that occur in a sales career when you fail to get a sale. Furthermore, you will learn if you truly like convincing people to buy a particular product.

$\mathcal{L}et's\ \mathcal{M}eet...$

$\mathcal{K}irk\ \mathcal{M}artin$
$Car\ Salesperson$

Kirk has been selling new cars for 8 years. He currently works at a Chrysler/ Plymouth dealership where his record for sales is 19½ cars in 1 month.

What first attracted you to a career in selling cars?

Frankly, I was motivated by the income. I'm only 25 years old now, and there are very few jobs in which I could make this much money without a college education.

Tell me how you got your first job.

It is difficult to get your first job because everyone wants you to have experience. I was lucky, however, to get hired at the second or third place where I applied because I had retail sales experience. Then a friend I had made while selling stereos was promoted to manager at another car dealership. He offered me a job that paid more money, so I went to that dealership and stayed there for 3 years.

How did you learn how to sell cars?

The first day the assistant sales manager taught me how to fill out finance forms and worked with me on the sales floor. There is not much training. You really need to meet someone who can be a role model or mentor to learn this business.

What do you like least about your job?

The long hours are the worst part of my job. I frequently work 12- and 15-hour days because I must suit my customers' needs.

What is the most difficult part of your job?

I find it hard to stay focused and motivated when I don't sell a car for a few days. I couldn't handle this job if I didn't set goals and try constantly to find more creative ways to sell cars. I read a lot of books on motivation and psychology and business and negotiating skills.

What do you see yourself doing 5 years from now?

I would like to have my own business. It could be related to my hobby of collecting saltwater fish. Fortunately, this is a good possibility because I am able to save enough money to have sufficient capital to open a business.

Kirk's First Day Selling Cars

You know how some people feel before they go to the dentist—absolutely terrified. That is exactly how I felt my first day selling cars. It was a "sink or swim" experience. The assistant sales manager showed me how to fill out finance forms, and then, before I knew what was happening, I was greeting my first customer. The customer told me he was just looking and not yet ready to buy. I was so inexperienced that I didn't realize that I needed to pursue the customer more aggressively or turn him over to a more experienced salesperson.

Although it seems impossible, I actually sold a car to my second or third customer with the help of the assistant sales manager, who worked with me part of the day. The customer came in and asked, "Where's your ad car?" The assistant manager told me which car it was. I showed the car to the customer who said that he would take it. The sale was that easy, and I had started my career selling cars.

Let's Meet...

Gwen Mustin
Car Salesperson

Gwen Mustin has been selling cars successfully since 1978. Her sales efforts have made her salesperson of the month several times and salesperson of the year at a Ford dealership.

What first attracted you to a career in car sales?

Family members sold cars and talked about cars all the time. I spent a lot of time at the dealership and would fill in when someone didn't show up as a secretary or phone operator, so I knew what being a salesperson was like.

Describe your first job.

I was the first woman ever hired at an Oldsmobile dealership where most of the salespeople had been there for years and had repeat customers. There was no training and few walk-in customers. I was simply told to find people and sell cars. I made a valiant effort by contacting everyone I knew, giving flyers to neighbors, and telling the people I met about my job in order to develop a circle of influence. Unfortunately, my efforts resulted in the sale of only three cars, so I did not stay with this job for long.

Tell me about your other jobs selling cars.

After my first discouraging experience, I went back to work in radio where I had worked before. Then after several moves across the country, I got another job selling cars. One day when I had been at this job for a short time, I went to a new car showing and met a group of very enthusiastic salespersons. I asked if there were job openings where they worked and got a job selling at this dealership that was selling cars like crazy. I was even given a Thunderbird to drive.

On the job at Ford dealerships, I have received continuous training. Ford wants salespeople who fully understand the product and wants you to make each customer a customer for life. When I first started selling, salespeople really didn't know a lot about cars. Now I can even tell you the type of foam that is used in the car cushions.

What type of sales incentives do you receive?

First of all, I work completely on commission, so I must sell cars to literally put food on the table. Ford also tests salespeople on their knowledge of cars. If you receive a perfect test score, you become certified to receive gifts—from monetary awards to the use of a car. Recently, I went to a showing, scored 100 percent on a test, and had the opportunity to participate in a drawing to use a car for a year. Also, customers send back surveys to Ford, which can lead to honors and job promotions.

Selling Cars Is a Great Job for Women

When I first started selling cars more than 15 years ago, there weren't very many women doing this job. Today, this has changed. Of course, this career has both advantages and disadvantages for women.

Advantages

- Many women have an ability to listen that helps them discern exactly what their customers want.
- Female customers often prefer to talk to you instead of a man. This is important because women play an important role in more than 60 percent of all car-buying decisions.
- Many women are very good at pointing out the appointments of a car and stressing its features as well as benefits.
- This career allows women to achieve financial independence and to raise a family.

Disadvantages

- Women more often than men have to prove that they can be successful car salespersons.
- Some people still harbor prejudice against women in the business world. Be prepared, but do not let it ruin your attitude or dampen your enthusiasm.

Success Stories

Lee Iacocca

One of the most well-known executives in the automobile industry, Lee Iacocca began his career as an engineer with the Ford Motor Company. He soon moved to sales, an area that he liked better. While at Ford, he was responsible for the successful development and launch of the Mustang, a very popular sports car. In 1970, Iacocca became president of the Ford Motor Company, but he was dismissed in 1978. He then went to work for the Chrysler Corporation. Iacocca helped turn around the nearly bankrupt corporation. He got the federal government to guarantee loans and got the company to make fuel-efficient cars and reduce spending. Iacocca became a household name through his personal appeal in TV advertisements for Chrysler. To learn more about Iacocca's dynamic career, read his autobiography.

Saturn

The Saturn car was conceived almost 12 years ago when General Motors Corporation (GM) decided to find the best way to manufacture and market automobiles. The Saturn is built almost entirely within its Spring Hill, Tennessee, plant, which is unusual for GM. Saturn's plant is also run with an emphasis on teamwork and good relations between labor and management. Saturn advertised the car by focusing on the buyer or Saturn employees' feelings about the car instead of just the car's qualities. And in selling the car, Saturn has introduced a set price and eliminated the typical negotiations between salespeople and customers.

Find Out More

You and automobile sales

Not every person is suited to be an automobile salesperson. To see if you have the skills and qualities of most good automobile salespeople, check this list:

1. You are a high school graduate.
2. You received good grades in math, business, psychology, and speech courses.
3. You are a skillful driver.
4. You enjoy learning about and sharing your knowledge of the latest technology and design developments for automobiles.
5. You like working with people and are a friendly person.
6. You have nice manners and personal appearance.
7. You enjoy the challenge of matching a person's desires with the right product.
8. You are not upset by rejection.
9. You like to talk with people whom you don't know.
10. You are a hard-working, self-motivated person.
11. You have had some experience in selling.
12. You are a good negotiator and persuader.

The more of these skills and qualified you possess, the better suited you are to a career in automobile sales.

Find out more about selling new and used automobiles

To learn more about selling cars, you will want to contact these organizations for career information:

National Automobile Dealers
  Association
8400 Westpark Drive
McLean, VA 22102

National Independent Automobile
  Dealers Association
2521 Brown Boulevard
Arlington, TX 76006–5203

National Association of Fleet
  Resale Dealers
1484 South Reeves, Suite 101
Los Angeles, CA 90035

You can become knowledgeable about cars by reading car magazines such as *Car and Driver, Road & Track,* and *Motor Trend.*

CAREERS IN TEACHING DRIVER INSTRUCTION

J ust about everyone wants to learn to drive. Become a driving instructor, and you will work with teen-agers eager to get driver's licenses, older people who have never learned how to drive, and licensed drivers who want to upgrade their driving skills. You will help your students solve the riddle of parallel parking, teach them how to enter and exit freeways, and, above all else, instruct them in safe driving practices. As a driving instructor, there is also the exciting possibility of teaching racing techniques, stunt driving, and high-performance driving.

What it's like to be a driving instructor

Your job is not dangerous. You will be able to anticipate what a beginning driver is going to do because new drivers do the same things. And for safety, you will have a brake and may even have a gas pedal and wheel. Besides teaching people how to drive, you may spend part of your time in the classroom teaching a group of students about cars, traffic safety, and state driving laws. Some instructors choose to spend all of their time teaching the classroom phase of driver instruction. You are more likely to do this if you teach at a high school. At a commercial driving school, most driving instructors will spend more time in a car than in a classroom.

Let's find out what happens on the job

You will usually drive up to each student's home in a dual-controlled car. Your driving session will last from 1 to 2 hours. During that time, you will concentrate on teaching your student what is needed to pass the state's driving test. Because every one of your students will have different needs, you will have to adapt and personalize your instruction to each new driver. By the end of the day you will have spent from 8 to 10 hours with students.

The pleasures and pressures of the job

It is a pleasure to be your own boss and determine exactly how you will teach each student. And you are always meeting new people with diverse backgrounds. Imagine working in just one day with a high school junior, a lady who has just arrived from India, and a retired banker. Furthermore, you are never bored with the scenery because it changes throughout the day as you drive on different streets and highways. Of course, there are times when the weather is so bad your lessons are cancelled, and you aren't able to earn as much money. And you can't dictate your work hours because you must work when your students are free.

The pay and the perks

If you work for a commercial driving school, your pay will probably be by the hour. Depending on where you work, you will earn from $7 to $15 per hour. Full-time employees usually receive health benefits and paid vacation. They rarely receive sick days or retirement benefits. There is a new trend for driving instructors to become independent contractors. In this case, the instructor owns the training car and may work for more than one driving school. If you work for a high school, your pay scale will be the same as the other teachers. In the early 1990s, this averaged more than $30,000 a year. High school instructors also receive health care, paid vacations, and retirement benefits.

Getting started

Driving instructors working at high schools must be college graduates and certified by the state in driver education. To work as a driving instructor at a commercial school, you need a special license in most states. Although requirements vary, you usually have to be 21 years old and a high school graduate. Successful applicants will pass both written and driving tests. They may also be required to pass a physical examination and a background check for criminal and traffic records. Quite often instructors also have to take formal driver instruction courses at colleges. To even apply for an instructor's license, it is frequently necessary to be sponsored by a driving school that will hire you after you receive a license. After you are hired and have a license, most schools will give you some on-the-job training.

Climbing the career ladder

There are approximately 3,500 driving schools in the United States at the present time, and 2,500 of these schools are one-car operations. The owner is typically the instructor as well as the business manager. Before driving instructors start their own schools, they usually work at a driving school. Depending on the size of the school, driving instructors can climb the career ladder to become a supervisor, an office manager, and then possibly the owner.

Now decide if being a driving instructor is right for you

Think about all the teachers you have in school right now. Would you like to do their job? Of course, most of the time driving instructors at commercial schools teach in a car rather than a classroom. Still, as a driving instructor, you are likely to do some classroom instruction. In many states, teenagers must take 30 hours of classroom instruction. When you teach this class, the curriculum will come from the state. However, you will have to make assignments, give lectures, and arrange for videos and filmstrips. If you teach driver's education at a high school, you may also teach other subjects. Before deciding on a career as a driving instructor, remember you are deciding on a career as a teacher.

Let's Meet...

Bob Maxino
Driving School Owner

Bob is a driving instructor who became an owner of the largest driving school in the United States. He also is past president of the Driving School Association of the Americas, Inc.

What first attracted you to a career in driving instruction?

When I was in the insurance business and doing a lot of traveling, I saw a great number of accidents and near accidents. I also noticed many bad drivers on the road. While on vacation, I saw a driver training car and decided then and there that I wanted to have a job that involved improving drivers.

Did you need any special schooling or training?

I received training from the driving school where I was going to be an instructor. I saw films and went out in a car for about a week with an instructor while he was teaching students.

What special skills do you need to be a good driving instructor?

You need to be an excellent driver. You must also have the ability to establish a good rapport with different people.

What do you learn on the job?

You grow with every student. The longer you teach driving, the better you are. You learn how people react to what you say. Eventually, you accumulate a reservoir of knowledge. For example, the first time you encounter a problem, you may experiment. With experience, you learn how to solve most problems.

Is there a lot of competition for jobs as a driving instructor?

If you are qualified, you should be able to find a job. Many people fancy becoming a driving instructor but lose interest after finding out how much time, money, and effort are required.

What advice would you give young people starting out in driver instruction?

You must be willing to go through the complicated process of obtaining a license. You must also realize that you are making a commitment to work hours when others are free. More and more students learning to drive are teenagers, and during the school year they are free only after school and on weekends. You are also choosing a career where you will work long hours. Sixty-hour weeks are quite common. And you may find that you have to begin at 7:00 a.m. and not quit until 10:00 p.m. Be sure that you will enjoy this career.

How Bob Became a Leader in Driving Instruction

Bob started out as a driving instructor at the school where he now is a co-owner. For 10 years, he worked as an instructor, then he became the office manager. This involved setting up all the drivers' schedules, managing the phone operation, and hiring, firing, and training driving instructors. Ten years ago, the owner of the school retired. Bob and another employee became co-owners; she handles the financial side of the school, which has grown into the largest school in the United States.

Bob's time is not just spent at his school. As a past president of the Driving School Association of the Americas, Inc., he presents seminars to school owners on instructor training, advertising, buying cars, and managing a business. Bob says this organization has a tremendous responsibility as the educator of most teen drivers because schools have cut back on offering driver education. He is working hard to ensure that commercial driving schools offer quality instruction.

Let's Meet...

Howard Halterman
Driving Instructor

Howard is an instructor at the Bob Bondurant School of High Performance Driving where he specializes in teaching stunt and security driving techniques.

Is a career in driving instruction something you always dreamed of?

I always wanted to be involved in racing. As a kid, I watched races at the Sears Point Raceway in Northern California. The Bondurant Driving School was there, and I knew that I wanted to go through it.

How did you know that you would enjoy working as a driving instructor at Bondurant?

Racing is in my blood. I have been a motocross racer and am now racing go-carts. At Bondurant, driving instructors have the opportunity to spend time out on the track testing cars and perfecting their high-speed driving techniques.

How did you get started in driver instruction?

I accepted a job working in the shop at the Bondurant School just to get my foot in the door. I knew I could climb the company ladder with hard work.

What classes do you teach?

I started teaching a one-day Defensive Driving Course. Then I taught a 2/3-day High Performance Driving Course. Now I teach all the courses offered at the school.

What do you like most about your job?

The adrenaline—from high-speed driving and riding with others. There are no dual-control cars for Bondurant driving instructors.

What do you like least about your job?

Hot days and when students crash. There are almost no injuries at the school because safety is stressed.

What are some of the safety features?

Both the instructor and the student are really harnessed in like they were in a race car. We wear four-point harnesses and safety helmets. The cars have window nets, fire systems, roll bars, and fuel cells that don't rupture.

Do you get to meet a lot of new people on the job?

I meet new people every course. A lot of celebrities take these courses. Most of my students come for fun and fantasy.

What is the most difficult part of your job?

You have to maintain 110 percent concentration when you are doing this type of driving. It is hard to do so for long periods of time.

A Day Teaching Stunt Driving

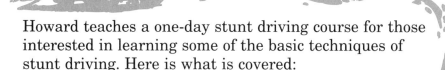

Howard teaches a one-day stunt driving course for those interested in learning some of the basic techniques of stunt driving. Here is what is covered:

Classroom Session (1 hour)—Basic driving techniques are reviewed.

Basic Techniques and Slalom Course (45 minutes)— In the car, the instructor demonstrates the physics involved in driving. The student learns how the throttle affects car handling and drives through a slalom course to introduce the basic concepts of vehicle control, including smoothness and weight transfer.

Accident Avoidance (1 hour)—Students are taught split-second car control during emergency evasive maneuvers and controlled braking and panic stops that could save their lives.

Race Track Driving (2 hours)—The students put driving techniques together at higher speeds.

Parking Lot (1–3 hours)—Students practice maneuvers such as high-speed spins and how to put a car where a director wants it.

At the conclusion of the course, students still need loads of practice on their own to truly become stunt drivers.

Success Stories

Bob Bondurant

For more than 26 years, students have been receiving driving instruction at the Bob Bondurant School of High Performance Driving. Founded in 1968, the school has instructed more than 50,000 students. Graduates include teenagers, housewives, and executives, as well as celebrities like Tom Cruise, Clint Eastwood, and Candice Bergen, and race drivers like Rick Mears, Davey Allison, and Dale Earnhardt.

Before Bob Bondurant started his school, he was a successful race car driver. He had grown up with a passion for anything on wheels and was racing motorcycles on dirt ovals by the time he was 18. Then he started driving sports cars, winning many races, like the GT category at the prestigious LeMans. His expertise was recognized with awards, including the Corvette Driver of the Year Award. Bob also raced Formula One cars successfully.

A serious racing accident in 1967 forced Bob to think about the future. He decided to open up a driving school and use his experience and expert knowledge of driving to teach others how to be better drivers. Today, Bob's school is at the forefront of professional driving instruction. Courses range from Teenage Defensive Driving and High Performance Driving to Grand Prix Racing.

Whenever he has time, Bob teaches. He also travels across the country promoting safe and advanced driving skills as a consumer advisor to Ford. And he still continues to race—only now the races are in vintage and historic automobile events.

Find Out More

You and driver's education

To have a successful career as a driver's education instructor you must be an excellent, responsible, and safe driver. Educate yourself on what safe driving habits are, and then practice them whenever you are driving. Even if you don't pursue a career as a driver's education instructor, you will have become a better and safer driver.

Now, answer the following questions to see if you possess the teaching skills and qualities of a driver's education instructor. Also, give an example of a situation in your life that applies to each question and explain how you felt.

1. Can you give instructions so that they are easily understood and followed?

2. Are you able to assess a person's ability and give suggestions for improvement?

3. Can you develop a well-thought-out lesson plan?

4. Do you remain calm in tense driving situations?

5. Do you like working with people and helping them to learn?

If your answers were "yes," and you have had good driving experiences, then a career as a driver's education instructor may be right for you.

Find out more about being a driving instructor

Find out what it is like to be a driving instructor by contacting a local driving school if you want to work for a private school. If you want to teach driver's education at a high school, talk to a high school instructor and find out what a day or a week is like in the life of a driving instructor. You may also be able to obtain helpful career information from these organizations.

American Automobile Association
1000 AAA Drive
Heathrow, FL 32746–5063

National Safety Council
1121 Spring Lake Drive
Itasca, IL 60143–3201

CAREERS IN

REPAIRING

CARS

More cars are on the road every year. Although more reliable than ever before, cars still break down and need to be repaired and also require routine service to keep them running smoothly. Thousands of cars are also damaged in traffic accidents every day. More than one million auto mechanics, often called "automotive service technicians," as well as automotive body repairers are currently working to keep about 150 million passenger cars and taxis operating in the United States.

What it's like to be an auto mechanic

Because cars have become so complex, you will probably specialize in an area such as engine repair, brakes, collision damage repair, transmission, or electrical systems. On the job, you will use the thousands of dollars of equipment you have accumulated over the years, plus the power tools, engine analyzers, and other test equipment that your employer furnishes. Your workplace will be indoors, and it is likely to be quite noisy if you are a body repairer. You will probably work at an automobile dealer, independent repair shop, or gasoline service station. Only 20 percent of automotive mechanics and body repairers are self-employed.

Let's find out what happens on the job

Auto mechanics typically get a description of a problem from the customer or the service adviser. Then the mechanic must figure out exactly what the problem is. This frequently involves using a wide variety of electronic equipment to assist in making the correct diagnosis. You may even have to test drive the car. After the problem is determined, it is time to fix it. This involves repairing or replacing one or more of the faulty parts. Not all your work will be repair work, you will also do routine maintenance work such as lubrication and changing oil. You will not fix dents, straighten bent fenders, or replace broken glass; this job is usually done by body repairers.

The pleasures and pressures of the job

You are faced with challenging problems. Perhaps you have to find out why a car suddenly hesitates after it has been running for an hour, or why an engine has to be cranked repeatedly the first time it is started. Solving problems like these is one of the greatest satisfactions of being an auto mechanic.

You may find some of the physical aspects of being an auto mechanic unpleasant. You are going to get your hands dirty. Frequently, you'll skin your knuckles. You are going to find yourself in awkward and cramped positions. Furthermore, your work will be strenuous at times when you lift heavy parts and tools.

The rewards, the pay, and the perks

Being an auto mechanic or body repairer is very rewarding because each day you can clearly see what you have accomplished. You see cars leaving your shop in perfect running order or with all their dents removed. How much you earn as an auto mechanic or body repairer is determined largely by your skill level. You may not earn much more than $9 an hour if you are a semi-skilled mechanic. A highly skilled mechanic or body repairer, however, can earn more than $50,000 a year. And if you work more than 40 hours in a week, you will receive overtime.

Getting started

The number of skills needed to be a skilled auto mechanic is constantly growing. You can still start by working as a trainee mechanic, helper, lubrication worker, or gas station attendant and gradually acquire skills by working with experienced mechanics. This approach is discouraged by most training authorities. You can also enter a 3- or 4-year apprenticeship program, but the number of these programs is getting smaller.

Formal automotive training programs have increased in popularity. According to the experts, the best route to becoming an auto mechanic is to take a formal training program at a community college, vocational school, or technical school. Find a program that is certified by the National Automotive Technicians Education Foundation (NATEF).

Climbing the career ladder

You will advance through several steps until you become a skilled, advanced technician. Then it will be possible to continue climbing the career ladder to shop supervisor or service manager. Or you could take a different route and become a service consultant and work with customers. You could even decide to open your own repair shop.

Now decide if being an auto mechanic is right for you

Auto mechanics are highly skilled professionals. They need to constantly update their skills. For example, electronics knowledge was once only essential for those working on engine controls and dashboard instruments. Today, electronics are being used in brakes, transmissions, steering systems, and a variety of other components. Most auto mechanics must now be familiar with the basic principles of electronics to recognize when an electronic malfunction may be the cause of a problem. Are you willing to attend seminars and clinics and read trade publications and technical manuals to constantly learn new skills? You will have to do this to remain a top-notch mechanic.

Things you can do to get a head start

You must graduate from high school. While you are in school, you can get a head start by studying automotive repair, electronics, physics, chemistry, and mathematics. Experience working on cars in the Armed Forces or as a hobby can also be valuable. Begin now to contact associations to get information on training programs and job qualifications.

Let's Meet...

Dave Bretones
Driveability and Electrical Technician

Dave has been working on cars since he was 13. He is a master technician and a member of the Buick Advisory Council—the top 25 Buick technicians in the country.

What first attracted you to a career as an auto mechanic?

Our church had a program that taught young people how to tune cars to make money for summer activities. I started to tune cars at 13 and was immediately drawn to this career. When I was 14, I bought a car, took the engine apart, and put it back together.

Tell me how you got started working in car repair.

While in high school, I repaired teachers' cars and worked on the cars of family and friends. After graduation, I worked at a gas station where I pumped gas for 2 years before I started repairing cars. Then I applied for an opening as an apprentice mechanic at a new Buick dealership and got the job.

Did you need any special schooling or training?

For 4 years I worked with a journeyman technician learning every area of car repair. I worked a 40-

hour week and went to class two nights a
week to study auto repair subjects. To
become a journeyman mechanic, you must
have a certain number of hours of classwork
in several areas.

Have you had any other classes or training?

I have attended classes at the General
Motors Training Center. I have also partici-
pated in the Buick Service Master's
Program. You study service bulletins all year
and do your own research. Then you take
tests and are certified at one of four levels. I
am a member of the Advisory Council, which
is the highest level.

Describe a typical day at work.

I work from 7:30 a.m. to 4:30 p.m. with an
hour for lunch. The dispatcher gives me my
work assignments. Here is what I did on a
recent day:

> Replaced an alternator.
>
> Went to a customer's home to observe a
> starting problem.
>
> Did three tuneups.
>
> Spent 2 hours solving an electrical
> problem on a car.
>
> Worked on an air conditioner.
>
> Did a smog inspection.

Dave Is a Master Automobile Technician

Dave has a plaque on the wall in his work station identifying him as a Master Automobile Technician. This means he has passed eight tests in the Automobile Technician certification program of The National Institute for Automotive Service Excellence (ASE) and has at least 2 years of hands-on work experience in automotive repair. By passing these tough, national tests, Dave has shown that he is among the elite in his profession. He has the credentials to prove his competence to his customers, coworkers, and employers. According to Dave, earning this certificate brought him a great deal of personal satisfaction.

The ASE was founded in 1972 to improve the quality of automotive service and repair. It offers a series of eight tests for automobile/light truck repair professionals. Technicians who pass all eight tests, as Dave did, become an ASE Master Automobile Technician. Certified technicians must retake the examination at least every 5 years for recertification.

Let's Meet...

Ted Mendelson
Body Repair Shop Owner

Ted has repaired, restored, and painted car bodies from family cars to exotic prize winning show cars.

What first attracted you to a career in auto-body repair?

My decision to become an auto-body repair technician was not a swift one. After high school, I went to four different colleges and majored in a different subject at each school. Then I took some time off and traveled and thought about what I wanted to do. I reached back and remembered how I had loved building a go-cart when I was 12, plus how much I had liked art school. Then I knew that body repair was right for me because it combined both building and painting.

Did you need any special schooling or training?

I went to a community college for 2 years and earned a certificate of completion in auto body and fender. Five hours a day for 5 days a week I had hands-on experience with cars; only an hour a day was spent in the classroom. Later, I took classes and earned certification in all aspects of collision repair.

Trace your career path.

While I was in school, I worked part-time at a company that made fiberglass kit car bodies. I helped design and make molds and did a show paint job on the owner's prototype car. I worked there the summer after getting my certificate, then I worked in a body repair shop for 6 years that specialized in restoring exotic show cars. Next, for $1\frac{1}{2}$ years, I worked at three large body shops as a journeyman auto painter. Then I started looking for my own shop. I began as a one-man operation, and today—14 years later—I have six employees in my auto-body repair shop. Although most of my time is spent on managerial responsibilities, I still work on cars occasionally.

Describe the work environment in your shop.

Auto-body work can be dangerous. When you are doing body work, you are using drills and cutting torches and welding tools. When you paint, you are working with paints that are poisonous. We are very conscious of safety in my shop. Ear protectors are worn for loud operations; protective goggles are used when necessary, as are dust masks. The painter uses a fresh air respirator when painting.

In your body shop, do people work alone or as part of a team?

In most shops, work is departmentalized into body work and paint work. Typically, one person will assemble and disassemble a car, and another person will do the painting and priming.

Ted's Career Highpoint

In California, a premier yearly event, the Concours d'Elegance, is held at Pebble Beach. High-quality and high-interest show cars in the West that were built before 1940 are exhibited. The majority are from the 1930s. You can't just exhibit in this show; your car has to be accepted into the show.

At the end of the show, the owners of the winning cars drive up a ramp and accept a trophy. One year at the show the announcer asked the owner of a certain Ferrari to go over to the car. It was the car that I had painted. I rushed over to the owner and told him that he was going to win the prestigious Hans Tanner Award, which is given for the favorite Ferrari race car at the show. I was so excited that the owner invited me to ride the car up the ramp with him. I was photographed in the car with the owner accepting the award. This is the most recognition that I ever got in this show, and I am still very proud of being a part of restoring this magnificent car.

Success Stories

A.J.
Foyt

A.J. Foyt is one of the greatest American race car drivers. He has thrilled racing fans for almost 40 years. Foyt grew up in Houston, Texas, learning how cars operated from his father, an auto mechanic and midget car racer. Foyt developed a reputation as a master of driving and mechanics perfection. He raced and won in dirt cars, midgets, sprint cars, championship cars, Indy cars, stock cars, and sports cars. Among his many wins were a record-setting four Indy 500 victories.

Pep
Boys

Manny, Moe, and Jack (who was later replaced by Izzy) began their business in 1921 with one retail auto parts store in Philadelphia. Today, there are more than 370 Pep Boys Automotive Supercenters in 25 states, and the chain is still expanding. Pep Boys is primarily geared to sell auto parts to those customers who want to do their own repairs. Pep Boys also has service centers that will do most repair jobs for you.

Find Out More

You and repairing cars

Now you need to decide if a career in repairing and/or servicing automobiles is right for you. Take this quiz to see if you have some of the basic qualities and interests of a good repairer or service technician.

1. Do you spend your free time tinkering with cars or reading car magazines?
2. Does it bother you to get dirty?
3. Do you like to work with your hands? Are you any good at it?
4. Do you have a good understanding of how automobiles work?
5. Do you have an aptitude for mechanics?
6. Do you enjoy solving problems?
7. Do you keep working at a problem until it is solved?
8. Are you willing to keep up with new technology and learn new repair and/or service methods?
9. Can you explain technical issues to customers in an easy-to-understand manner?

**Find out
more about
repairing
cars**

You may wish to begin learning about a career in repairing cars by contacting these associations:

National Automotive Technicians
    Education Foundation
13505 Dulles Technology Drive
Herndon, VA 22071–3415

Automotive Service Association
1901 Airport Freeway, Suite 100
P.O. Box 929
Bedford, TX 76021–0929

For information on two-year associate degree programs in automotive service technology, contact:

ASSET Program
Training Department, Room 109
Ford Parts and Service Division
3000 Schaefer Road
Dearborn, MI 48121

Chrysler Dealer Apprenticeship
    Program
National CAP Coordinator
CIMS 423-21-06
26001 Lawrence Avenue
Center Line, MI 48015

General Motors Automotive
    Service Educational Program
National College Coordinator
General Motors Service
    Technology Group
30501 Van Dyke Avenue
Warren, MI 48090

CAREERS IN DRIVING A BUS OR TAXI

I magine spending your day behind the wheel of a motor vehicle. If you really like to drive, being a bus or taxi driver could be just the right career for you. As a bus or taxi driver, you will be a true people mover, helping people get where they want to go. There are many exciting career possibilities. You could be driving the same route all day, driving short or long distances between cities—even states, or driving to different places throughout the day. You could be working for a private company, a school district, or a municipality.

What it's like to be a driver

As a bus or taxi driver, you will find yourself operating a vehicle in all kinds of traffic and weather conditions. You are responsible for the safety of your passengers and others. You need to keep alert to prevent accidents and try not to stop or swerve suddenly.

Bus drivers usually follow a fixed route and time schedule. Local transit bus drivers work 5 days a week. Many work split shifts where they drive in the morning, have several hours off, and drive again in the late after-noon to accommodate commuters. Intercity bus drivers may work almost anytime of the day or night. Unlike bus drivers, taxi drivers do not follow a fixed schedule. They usually try to design their workday around the times that people need rides, like rush hours.

Let's find out what happens on the job

Bus drivers usually begin their day by picking up their buses at garages or terminals. Before start-ing a route, drivers carefully inspect the bus. They check things like the bus' tires, brakes, safety equipment, lights, fuel, oil, and water. Beside picking up and dropping off passengers, drivers usually have to collect fares and may have to handle luggage. And of course, they also must answer their passengers' questions. At the end of the day, they complete reports. If you are a taxi driver, you will get your passengers from dispatchers, cab stands, or places where passengers are likely to be.

The pleasures and pressures of the job

One of the main pleasures of the job is being able to do something you truly enjoy—driving. You will meet a lot of different people and experience changing scenery during your workday. If you like being independent, it can be a great joy to have responsibility for your vehicle and its passengers, as well as working unsupervised most of the time.

On the other hand, bad traffic and/or weather conditions can make driving very stressful. You may feel pressured to hurry as a bus driver because you are falling behind schedule or as a taxi driver because a passenger wants to get somewhere quickly. At times, passengers may be difficult or distracting. Also, there is the possibility of the bus or taxi being robbed.

The rewards, the pay, and the perks

Local transit and school bus drivers receive hourly wages; however, intercity bus drivers are usually paid by the number of miles driven, not hours. Generally, bus drivers will get health and life insurance, sick and vacation leave, and free bus rides, but school bus drivers to not get vacation leave. Also, many bus drivers become members of a union, which affects their pay and benefits.

Taxi drivers' earnings depend on such things as how long they work, how they get paid, and what season it is. Many taxi drivers are paid a percentage of their total fares collected. They also receive tips from passengers.

Getting started

To be a bus driver you will have to meet many federal, state, and local requirements dealing with personal and professional qualifications and standards. Federal regulations demand that you obtain a commercial driver's license for the state in which you live if you operate a vehicle that carries 16 or more passengers. Most employers prefer their bus drivers to have a high school education and good reading and writing skills.

To be a taxi driver, usually you will need to have a taxicab operator's license and a chauffeur's license. To obtain these licenses, you will probably have to pass written and driving tests. Most employers prefer their taxi drivers to have at least an eighth-grade education.

Climbing the career ladder

After successful completion of the training program, new intercity and local transit bus drivers may be placed on an extra list and drive only when full-time drivers can't. Full-time drivers can negotiate for more desirable routes and pay. There are not a lot of opportunities for advancement. Intercity and local transit bus drivers may become supervisors, dispatchers, or managers. School bus drivers may become fleet supervisors or driving instructors.

There are not many advancement possibilities for taxi drivers. They may be promoted to dispatcher, road supervisor, or garage superintendent. Some taxi drivers advance by buying their own cabs and going into business for themselves.

> **Now decide if driving a bus or taxi is right for you.**

To be a driver, you must be in good physical health, have 20/40 vision with or without correction, have good hearing, and be able to read, write, and speak English. Now, think about your answers to these questions carefully. How truly interested are you in driving? Would you like to spend your workday behind the wheel of a vehicle? Can you follow complex schedules and routes or find the best route to get somewhere? If you are not really excited about driving, then you might want to look at other chapters in this book that do not involve so much driving.

Let's Meet...

Debbie Walton
Bus Driver

Debbie started her career driving a school bus because she had two children and liked the idea that her work would fit around their schedules. She now drives a municipal bus.

Did you need any special schooling or training?

I had 10 hours of classroom time to learn the ins and outs of driving a school bus. Then an instructor taught me how to drive a bus. No students were on the bus while I was learning to drive. I also had to learn how to bleed the brakes and do the bus checkout list both before and after my route.

Did you have to get a special license?

In my state, you need what is called a Class B license to drive a bus. To get this license, I had to spend time in class, learn first aid, and take both a written test and a driver's test.

What do you like most about your present job driving for a municipality?

- Being on my own except when I have to connect with other buses.
- Seeing my regular passengers every day.

- Having good benefits—medical and dental insurance, paid vacations, and retirement.

What do you like least about this job?

- Being stuck in traffic.
- Dealing with passengers who don't have fares.
- Worrying that older passengers will fall.
- Handling the stress of always being on guard while driving.

Is there a lot of competition for jobs driving a bus?

Yes. When I started driving 13 years ago, part-time drivers could become full-time drivers in 3 months or even less. Today, it takes part-time drivers up to 3 years to go full time. Drivers simply don't leave their jobs.

What is your next career move likely to be?

I have been driving a bus now for almost 17 years. I love my job, but I'm ready for a new challenge. I would like to go into management and become a supervisor.

What It's Like To Drive Route 122

I drive a loop that takes 45 minutes to complete. At the end of each loop I usually have a break for 5 to 10 minutes. Occasionally, I have 15 minutes. I grab a bite to eat when I have the time.

My day starts at 6 a.m. when I check my bus to be sure it's safe to go on the road. I check the brakes, lights, windshield wipers, tires, and fire extinguisher. Then I do a walk-around, looking over the entire bus. To keep a record of my workday, I punch in the route number, my employee number, and the run number in the little computer aboard my bus.

My day ends at 3:30 p.m. when I take my bus back to headquarters. I punch out of the computer, check the bus for damage, and write out a report if anything needs to be fixed.

Let's Meet...

Alex Villasenor
Taxi Driver

Alex is a unique taxi driver because he drives a minivan instead of a car. He started as a part-time driver and now drives full-time in a suburban community.

Tell me about your first day at work.

Believe it or not, I started on New Year's Eve about 5:00 p.m. and didn't get off until 5:00 a.m. The party atmosphere was great.

Did you need any special permits or licenses?

When I first started working as a taxi driver, you needed to get a permit from the city. This is no longer true. You don't need a special license in my state, but you do need to be fingerprinted and have a good driving record.

Describe a typical day.

My day starts about 8:00 a.m. when I turn on my radio and start getting calls from the dispatcher. I'm real busy at first with the morning rush. Then around lunchtime, it slows down. I get busy again at the end of the day. I usually quit between 4:00 and 5:00 p.m. I get quite a few long hauls to the airport because the minivan has room for seven

passengers. I also act as a delivery courier at times.

What special skills do you need to be a good taxi driver?

Obviously, you have to be a good driver and like driving. But more than that you have to be a mini-psychiatrist. You would be surprised at the number of people who tell you their life story in 15 minutes. It is also important to have a good sense of humor. You have to be able to get along well with all kinds of people. And you can't get frustrated and angry because you are driving in heavy traffic.

Tell me about one of your most unusual passengers.

A man had a fight with his wife and asked me to take him home, which was 200 miles away (my longest haul ever). He didn't have the money to pay me at the start of the trip but promised to pay me when he reached home. I really thought he would pay me so I drove him home. When we reached his house, he went into the house and came back with the fare.

What is the most difficult part of your job?

This job doesn't lead anywhere. There is no possibility of advancement. I find this frustrating because I am ambitious.

What do you see yourself doing in the future?

I would like to have my own business

Things I Like and Dislike about My Job

I like my job because:

- It is different every day. It is never routine.
- I don't see the same people every day. At the same time, I have a few regular customers whom I enjoy.
- I help a lot of elderly people, which makes me feel good.
- The scenery is always changing. One day I may work on the west side of town. Another day, I work all over the town or make trips to the airport.
- I earn a good income.

I dislike my job because:

- There are no benefits.
- Many people do not regard it highly as a career.
- There is so much traffic, but it no longer stresses me out.

Success Stories

Greyhound Lines, Inc.

Two intercity bus operators, Orville Caesar and Eric Wickman, formed Motor Transit Management by merging several bus firms in the mid-1920s. Through buying companies and creating new lines, they were able to establish a network of bus lines crisscrossing the United States. Later, Motor Transit Management was renamed Greyhound Corporation. The greyhound racing dog, known for its sleek figure and great speed, became the firm's trademark. Today, Greyhound is a leader in intercity bus transportation service in the United States and Canada.

Taxicabs

The word *taxicab* comes from combining and shortening the words *taximeter* and *cabriolet*. The taximeter was a device invented by Wilhelm Bruhn to accurately calculate the distance traveled and the resulting fare. The cabriolet was a two-wheeled, horse-drawn carriage often used for hire. In the late 1800s, the first motorized cab was used in Paris, France. These cabs, in both Europe and the United States, ran on electric power. In 1907, the first gasoline-powered cab equipped with a taximeter was driven in New York City. The French used taxicabs during World War I to transport troops from Paris to the Marne. Today, a taxicab usually has a taximeter and is a four-door passenger car that's been altered somewhat to endure the heavy use.

Find Out More

You and driving a bus or taxi

If you have not recently taken a ride on the type of vehicle you are interested in driving, now is the time to do so. As you ride, pay close attention to the driver and the work environment. Think about whether that driver's job is one that you would like to have. After you ride, make up a list of what you observed. Be sure to include things like what the driver did, what challenges the driver faced, what rewards the driver received, and what kind of environment the driver worked in. Next, evaluate your list against what appeals to you in a career. If there is a good match, you could be on your way to a career as a driver.

See how you respond to these questions on the qualities of a successful driver:

1. Do you like driving?
2. Are you a good and safe driver in all types of weather?
3. Do you have steady nerves in tense situations?
4. Do you enjoy working with people?
5. Do you like to work alone, without direct supervision?

**Find out
more about
driving a
bus or taxi**

Through riding in buses and taxis, you will learn a great deal about a career driving these vehicles. Be sure to ask questions of these drivers when it is appropriate and safe to do so. Also, you will want to contact these organizations for more career information.

National School Transportation
　　Association
P.O. Box 2639
Springfield, VA 22152

American Public Transit
　　Association
1201 New York Avenue, NW
Suite 400
Washington, DC 20005

International Brotherhood of
　　Teamsters 1991
25 Louisiana Avenue, NW
Washington, DC 20001

CAREERS IN

ADJUSTING

CLAIMS

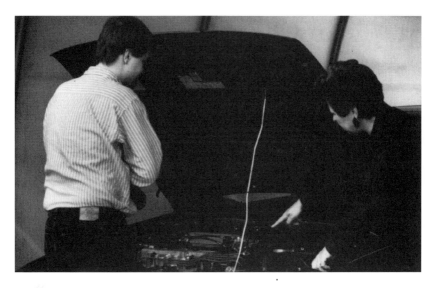

C ollisions! Crashes! Fender benders! With about 150 million cars on the road, it's no wonder that accidents are constantly occurring. And right in the center of seeing that people get their cars repaired and are compensated for injuries are more than 250,000 insurance claims representatives or adjusters, as they are also called. If you choose this career, you will be acting as an intermediary between insurance companies and clients who wish to receive money for their damaged vehicles or personal injuries.

What it's like to be a claims representative

Above all else, you will be a negotiator. You will negotiate the best price for repairs that you can get with auto and auto-body repair shops. You will negotiate with other insurance companies to determine how losses are to be shared. You will negotiate agreements that satisfy car owners. Besides being a negotiator, you will be an absolute car expert, knowing every part of a car and what is involved in fixing damaged cars. In addition to spending considerable time on the computer, you will also deal with a lot of paperwork.

Let's find out what happens on the job

You will be assigned claims by your office supervisor. You will find out, first of all, if the customer's insurance policy covers the loss. If you are an inside claims representative, your time will be spent on the phone contacting claimants and getting information on repair costs, medical expenses, and other details your company needs. You may also go outside and inspect cars to determine damage. Finally, you will negotiate settlements. If you are an outside claims representative, you will handle more complex cases, including visiting body shops, consulting police and hospital records, preparing reports for lawsuits, taking photographs, recording statements, and determining fault.

The pleasures and pressures of the job

Even though you follow the same steps to settle every claim, each day is different because you are working with new customers. Although you will be dealing with people who are quite stressed because they were involved in an accident or injured, you will be pleased that your work helps to reduce the stress they are suffering. At the same time, it can be upsetting to be constantly handling difficult customers. Some may become quite angry with you because they did not get the settlement they wanted. Furthermore, you may feel pressured because you have to handle a very high volume of cases.

The rewards, the pay, and the perks

As a claims representative, you will typically work a standard 5-day, 40-hour week. There may be some need to contact customers in the evening. If you are an outside claims representative, you will either use a company car or be reimbursed for using your own car. You will earn between $24,500 and $30,000 as an inside representative and from $28,500 to $36,500 as an outside representative. Your job should be fairly secure because the number of representatives needed does not fluctuate much.

Getting started

Most companies prefer to hire college graduates. However, companies will hire individuals without a college degree if they have knowledge of automobile mechanics or extensive clerical experience. No specific college major is recommended as preparation for a career as a claims representative. Courses in insurance, economics, and business could be helpful.

Many states require claims representatives, especially if they work for independent companies, to be licensed. Licensing typically involves taking specific state-approved courses and may also mean taking tests on the fundamentals of adjusting. After you are a claims representative, you will have to take continuing education courses in some states.

Climbing the career ladder

With on-the-job training and company-provided or continuing education courses plus experience, you can climb this career ladder:

inside claims representative

senior inside claims representative

outside claims representative

senior outside claims representative

claims examiner or technical specialist

supervisor

Now decide if being a claims representative is right for you

A career as a claims representative involves dealing with people. You must ask yourself these questions about your interpersonal skills and get a definite "yes" answer to each if this is the career for you:

Can I communicate effectively?

Can I handle disgruntled and angry customers?

Can I gain the respect and cooperation of others?

Things you can do to get a head start

The major thing you can do is to start learning about cars. Remember, in this career you are going to need an excellent knowledge of all the parts of a car. High school courses in auto mechanics can be a helpful starting point, so can reading about cars. You will also want to gain computer skills because much of your work as a claims representative will be done on the computer.

Let's Meet...

Gina Davis
Claims Representative

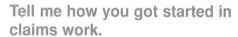

Gina has been a claims representative for an automobile insurance company for 6 years. Her job training included learning the names of every part of a car's body.

Tell me how you got started in claims work.

After 2 years of college, I took a summer job at my present company. The opportunity to get a job in claims appeared, and I never went back to college. Today, I would need to have a college degree to get the same starting job.

What special skills do you need to be a good claims representative?

First of all, you need to be a good negotiator. You spend much of your day trying to reach satisfactory agreements among body repair shops, car owners, and other insurers. Also, your communication skills need to be excellent because people may be quite stressed at having their cars damaged in an accident. And you have to have the ability to handle people who may not be receiving what they want in the settlement of a claim.

Describe a typical day at work.

My day begins at 8:30 a.m. when I arrive at the office. I gather my assignments and make phone calls to body shops to make sure vehicles are there and ready for inspection. By 9:00 I'm on the road in my company car to see the seven or eight cars that I evaluate each day. At each shop, I study the damaged car and then negotiate what needs to be done to put the car back in its original condition. At 3:00 p.m., I'm back in the office doing any necessary follow-up work and contacting the insured parties to let them know what is happening on their claims.

What do you like most about your job?

I like working with the people out in the field. I know all the body shop people so it is easy to negotiate with them. And I have very few problems.

What do you like least about your job?

It is very difficult to talk to people who have been in an accident where there was a fatality.

What is your next career move likely to be?

I started as an inside claims representative and was promoted to my current job as an outside claims representative. At the present time, I could move on to be a bodily injury specialist or a material damage examiner. I have decided to become an examiner when an opening comes up. This will involve a move away from the district office where I work now to the main office. The next step is material damage supervisor.

How I Learned To Be a Claims Representative

When I was hired to be a claims representative, I did not know too much more about a car than where the doors, bumper, and hood were. I certainly didn't know the difference between a fender and a quarter panel. The first day on the job, my supervisor gave me a picture of a car with all the parts named on it and told me to memorize them. From that day on, I went out into the parking lot by our office every day with an experienced inside claims representative to evaluate damaged cars. After 6 months of supervision which lessened as I gained expertise, I was on my own. After a year at this job, I felt that I really knew every part of the car.

Besides my daily training stints in the parking lot, I also learned how to answer phone calls, open a general report, take a recorded interview, diagram, negotiate with body repair shops, talk to the insured, and prepare files for lawsuits. I learned all these office procedures by working with experienced claims representatives and on-the-job training.

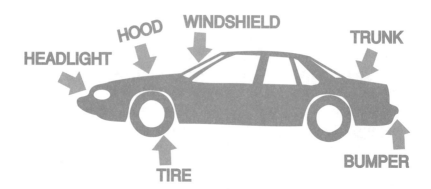

Let's Meet...

Sandra McKee
Insurance Broker

Sandra specializes in selling automobile insurance to nonstandard drivers who find it difficult to buy insurance because they are young, have a bad driving record, or are new to this country.

How did you know you would be successful selling automobile insurance?

I thought that I had the right type of personality for this job. When I was in high school, I took a career aptitude test and came out on the 99th percentile in persuasion. Besides, I had held several retail sales positions and been an effective salesperson.

Do you need a special license to sell automobile insurance?

In my state, you must have a license to sell insurance. When I first started out more than 10 years ago, you could take a crash course and then take the licensing test. Today, you have to have 60 hours of actual school training before you can take the test. Then every 2 years, you need to renew your license. To do this you need a certificate saying that you have taken so many hours of certified training. You can get the certificate by attending courses or studying at home through a correspondence school.

What special skills do you need to be a good insurance broker?

You need to be good with numbers. There is lots of math in this job. And it is essential that you are good at dealing with people.

What do you like most about your job?

This is one job in which women truly have the same opportunity as men to succeed. Also, it makes you feel good to be able to help people get the insurance protection they need. Some of the people I deal with can't get insurance at many companies.

What is the most difficult part of your job?

It's hard to deal with people who are not completely honest. When I ask someone about his or her traffic record, I figure the premium according to the risk. Then the insurance company runs a check of the driving record. If I have not been told the truth, he or she has to pay more.

What form of pay do insurance brokers receive?

In my present job, I work on a commission basis; however, in my previous job I received a salary plus a commission. Some brokers receive salaries only.

What is your next career move likely to be?

I plan to stay with this company because it is a small company that is expanding. I am being considered for the position of office manager.

My First Job as an Insurance Broker

I started working for an insurance company 10 years ago. This large company had a very thorough, formal training program. I had to complete a huge workbook, and the company actually gave me 2 to 3 hours each day to study at work. I could work at my own pace. When I completed a chapter, I would take a test and discuss the results with my supervisor.

After listening to other brokers make calls, I began to make "primary calls." I called people who had indicated they wanted insurance information. I would introduce myself, learn about their insurance needs, and set up an appointment to discuss their current policy. In the next calls, called "comparison calls," I explained the benefits and features of our company's plans and compared them to the customer's current policy. Few people have any idea of what insurance coverage they actually have or need. My biggest concern is to get people to get enough insurance to protect what they have.

Insurance Policy

Property Damage	10,000
Medical Payments	4,250
rehensive	125
on	550
Service	150
ehicle	15,000

to the office or
nvenient
ontact your

Insurance Policy

Property Damage	5,000
Medical Payments	4,000
Deductible Comprehensive	100
Deductible Collision	525
Emergency Road Service	50
Uninsured Motor Vehicle	10,000

Payment can be made to the office or
agent. For details on convenient
payment plans, please contact your
agent.

Insurance Policy

perty Damage	50,000
ical Payments	5,000
ctible Comprehensive	100
ctible Collision	500

Insurance Policy

Property Damage	10,000
Medical Payments	4,250
Deductible Comprehensive	125
Deductible Collision	550
Emergency Road Service	150
Uninsured Motor Vehicle	15,000

Payment can be made to the office or
agent. For details on convenient
payment plans, please contact your
agent.

Success Stories

American Automobile Association

The American Automobile Association (AAA) was founded in 1902. It is the world's largest travel organization with almost 34 million members. It is a group of automobile clubs whose main purpose is to make driving conditions better and to help its members with various automobile problems. AAA provides services such as insurance, emergency road repair, and assistance with travel plans. Also, AAA supports driver's education in high school and programs on automobile and traffic safety. The AAA has developed a book called *Sportsmanlike Driving* that provides information and projects to help you become a good driver.

The Indianapolis 500

The world's greatest sports spectacle is the Indianapolis 500, which is held each May. The original $2\frac{1}{2}$-mile rectangular racetrack was built in 1909 and paved with a mixture of stone and tar only to be covered with brick shortly afterwards. Today, only 3 feet of the brick track remain, the rest is paved over with asphalt. Besides providing racing excitement over the years, the track has been responsible for such automotive innovations as rearview mirrors and seat belts and has been the proving ground for front wheel drive, low-pressure tires, and hydraulic shock absorbers.

Find Out More

You and claims adjusting

See how you respond to these questions and comments about being a claims representative as you consider whether this is a career that appeals to you.

1. Are you interested in auto body repair and mechanics? You will need enough knowledge to assess the damage and determine the cost of repair.

2. Are you interested in insurance? You will need to be able to figure out if an insurance policy covers the damage and explain the details to your customer.

3. Are you familiar with using a computer? You will need to use a computer to record and keep track of your customer's claims.

4. Are you a good negotiator? You will need to negotiate the settlement of a claim that satisfies your customer and your insurance company.

5. Would you prefer to work out in the field or inside an office? You should start to think about this now because your career will be different depending on where you want to work.

**Find out
more about
adjusting
automobile
claims**

An excellent way to evaluate
whether you would like to be a
claims adjuster is by talking to
someone who is actively engaged
in this occupation. You will also
be able to get helpful career information from the following
organizations:

The Insurance Information
    Institute
110 William Street
New York, NY 10038

Alliance of American Insurers
1501 Woodfield Road
Suite 400 West
Schaumburg, IL 60173–4980

Insurance Institute of America
P.O. Box 3016
Malvern, PA 19355–0716

INDEX